PASS-I-ON

PASS-I-ON

7 BUILDING BLOCKS TO SUSTAINABILITY AND SUCCESS

Shawn M. Nicholson

L3 Publishing House L3 Life* Legacy* Legend

Contents

Dedication	vi
Photo Insert	1
Introduction	2
1 BUILDING BLOCKS TO SUSTAINABILITY AND SUCCESS	5
2 FAITH	8
3 FAVOUR	16
4 PASSION	22
5 RESILIENCE	40
6 REJUVENATION	47
7 REBRANDING	59
8 SUCCESS	70
Citations	79
About The Author	80

In memory of my late cousin Don Tuzo. Don was like an older brother to me. I decided to release my first book on his birthday **July 13.** Through the years, I have learned so much from him as an entrepreneur and we share a tremendous amount of similarities.

He wore this certain medallion. I never knew what it meant until he passed away. He truly was the definition of it, INTENSE! Everything he did, he was intense about it. Every deal, every idea, every conversation, every strategic plan, just intense. I now proudly wear this medallion.

So in memory of Don, I will carry on his legacy as well with my ability to **PASS-I-ON.**

Copyright © 2021 by Shawn M. Nicholson, for L3 Publishing House

All rights reserved. No portion of this book may be reproduced, stored in a retrieval system, or transmitted in any form or by any means—electronic, mechanical, photocopy, recording, scanning, or other—except for brief quotations in critical reviews or articles, without the prior written permission of the publisher. All citations are noted at the end of this book.

Published in North Chesterfield, Virginia by
L3 Publishing House
Post Office Box 74732
N. Chesterfield, Virginia 23236

ISBN: 978-0-578-94861-4

Cover layout and design by: Odaro Samuel Osakpolor
Author's photograph by: Nicole Brody Photography https://www.nicolebrody.co

For booking contact: booking@kingdombusiness.world

PASS—I-ON

7 BUILDING BLOCKS TO SUSTAINABILITY AND SUCCESS

Shawn M.
NICHOLSON

Introduction

Dear friend,

Thank you. You have just taken a bold step towards what will be a remarkable adventure.

I can't wait to announce your success to the world!

I am glad you picked up this book to read because that would mean, that like me, you are hungry for success. So, I am happy to have to you here, Welcome.

In this book, I will reveal the 7 building blocks that have helped me reach success. I am sure it would help you too, if you are dedicated to this course. Whatever you desire in life;

- Being financially free
- Living life on your terms
- The awe and respect of people who now doubt you
- A fresh beginning
- Just anything at all ….you will be able to attain it with these building blocks.

Reading this book in one sitting may only take you a few hours but the changes it will create in your life will be forever, and just like my life, it will bring a level of success and opportunity.

But first….

I want you to make me a very small promise.

Promise me that you will put whatever you have learned here into practice.

Here is what you need:

- A zeal to succeed
- Self-belief (because I do believe in you)
- Self discipline

Before we begin, permit me to brief you on my story; I believe you will be able to learn a few things from my life experiences. As PASS-I-ON, encompasses my step-by-step journey to success.

My name is **Shawn M. Nicholson** and I am an **Entrepreneur**. I am a third-generation entrepreneur on both my maternal and paternal side. I have always gravitated to business and wealth creation. My journey began as a son of a carpenter. I learned this trade from my father and it has provided everything that I could ever want for my family and I. I will admit, I learned it through default! I could recall being kicked out of school on many occasions and having to go to work with my father, which he and his brothers owned the company. As well as each of my summer vacations was spent working and learning vocational trades. I spent a great deal of time learning how to run crews and lead men and work with sub-contractors and vendors. In 1998, I pulled my father out of retirement and started my first official company S & M Nicholson Services. The first initials of my father and I, a gesture of appreciation. The company evolved and I changed the name to our parent company, Precise Business Group, Inc and opened satellite offices in 4 cities prior to the 2008 recession, making it until 2010. We were able to stand up a construction company, real estate development, home inspections under one brand. In 2016, we came back smarter, wiser and more driven and have been growing ever since. A business consulting firm, SMN Square, Inc, providing the building blocks for success and sustainability.

Of course, what I went through was not without challenges. I used to struggle with my age because I used to always be the youngest in the room. I didn't talk much but I observed a lot but when I did talk I commanded the room and had something to say. I grew up quick and was always around older people. My mother use to say that I was the oldest young person she knew. I cherish those experiences because it taught me wisdom and understanding. There is a scripture in the Bible explains that it is very notable to gain wisdom and one translation says wisdom is a principal thing but in all your getting get understanding. I am paraphrasing, of course, but the point is every challenge, obstacle, disappointment, I turned into a teachable moment.

Having access to capital or an inheritance was not available to me. However, I had a good foundation of knowledge. My dad was and is a remarkable role model. I had to do it the hard way and I am so grateful for that. As a result, each one of my businesses are debt free so I am able to reinvest in the businesses and start new businesses and create generational wealth for my family. L3 Life, Legacy, and Legend trademark we own.

Now, that's a peek into my story, summarized. While reading through this book, have it in mind that you are born to be great and no amount of challenges can stop you from achieving success if you have faith to begin with.

In case, you ever need my help. I am on each social media platform with the handle SMNSQUARE. Our website is www.smnsquare.com and my email address is Shawn@smnsquare.com

You can also connect with us on our weekly internet show Kingdom Business "Growing Ministry and Business" on the Power Network or visit www.kingdombusiness.world for more information.

1

BUILDING BLOCKS TO SUSTAINABILITY AND SUCCESS

BUILDING BLOCKS TO SUSTAINABILITY AND SUCCESS

Success, in any event, is made up of a collection of smaller events built on top of one another. Success is not, like some people think, luck. Through research, life experiences (the drive, the work ethics, the endurance, the knowledge, the experience), trial and error, I have found seven crucial building blocks that when applied can lead to success.

Success is not, like some people think, luck. You need to learn the basics first.

Basics To Success
1. HAVE A CLEAR GOAL

It is important to clearly define your goal so that you can repeat it to yourself. It should be short and concise, about seven words total. Make each word count. You will use this goal that you have created to check yourself to make sure that you are working towards it. Think big; don't hold back, anything is possible. No reason to limit yourself!

2. SMALL STEPS WORKING TOWARDS THE GOAL

This one seems pretty basic, but is worth mentioning. Once you have your goal, your mission, the thing that you are striving for, it may be overwhelming to try and tackle it in one big step. Goals are best achieved over a series of small steps, laying down a foundation which you can build upon. You'll notice that as you work towards your goal, it becomes easier because of the foundation that you have been building. This is true in anything you do, especially business.

3. CONSISTENCY

Just as small steps help you to get to your larger goal, being consistent is crucial for building on the steps that you have previously completed. Doing something small everyday will help you to form a habit.

4. PERSEVERANCE

Many people set their goals and start to work towards them, but as life throws curve balls, things change, time is consumed with other things and the consistency stops. It is absolutely important to persevere, stick with what you have set out to do, no matter what. The people that do persevere will achieve far more than those who stop and break the habits that they are forming. There is always time to do one small thing to work towards a goal. Time management becomes a top priority. Maybe you get up an hour earlier to work towards your goal, or maybe you stay up an hour later. Whatever you do, stick with it. It will pay off in the end.

5. REWARD YOURSELF FOR ACHIEVING YOUR GOAL- YOU DESERVE IT

When you have completed your goal, no matter how small it was, take time to reward yourself. Just like incentives work to sweeten a deal in a negotiation or when buying a product, or for completing a project on time at work, they work for yourself too. It doesn't have to be something extravagant, it could be purchasing a new album from iTunes or taking your mentors and advisers out to dinner to thank them for their support.

This is important to do as so many people work so hard but yet don't take the time to realize what they have accomplished. Many people have accomplished extraordinary things that go unnoticed. Take it upon yourself to reward yourself. You are your biggest fan, so make it happen. You deserve it.

After you celebrate, look at what you have accomplished and see where you want to go next. Set your next goal and build off of your success. It is a simple, continuous process.

6. PUT A TIME LIMIT TO YOUR GOAL

This one is important as you want to make sure you complete your goals, but you also don't want to stress yourself out to the point where you feel overwhelmed. Put a time limit on your goal, but do it in a realistic way. If you set a time limit and aren't finished with your goal then extend your time. One of the keys to life and to success is to be <u>flexible and adaptable</u>. Things will not always go as planned, so you need to be able to adapt to life and still complete what you set out to do.

It's now time for us to discuss the 7 building blocks to sustainability and success that I mentioned earlier one after the other;

1. Faith
2. Favor
3. Passion
4. Resilience
5. Rejuvenate
6. Rebranding
7. Success

2

FAITH

FAITH

Definitions Of Faith

Faith is the confidence or trust in a person, thing, deity, or in the doctrines or teachings of a religion or view (e.g. having strong political faiths). It can also be belief that is not based on proof.

Faith related to success

Having faith is one of the major requirements on the road to success. If you don't believe you can and will achieve what you intend to achieve it is virtually impossible to indeed achieve it.

Faith and belief

Although faith and belief seem to be the same thing, they have somehow a different 'feel' and are definitely not the same thing. To me, faith has a much more inspirational feel than belief. Belief seems to be 'just something one believes' and it may be right or wrong. While faith has something in it that you know you are going to achieve something because you believe you will.

The direct relationship between faith and success

The most successful humans are very faith-based humans.

Faith seems to most commonly be associated with religion. This ends up resulting in there being less discussion about faith in a secular sense. That's too bad. Faith is a great word expressing a powerful concept.

Consider this: No person without faith in himself, or others, has ever taken the leap to start a new business or set out on an adventure or learn something new or commit to a physical challenge or get married or attempt to make an impact in another person's life.

All these acts require faith in our abilities and faith in the abilities of others.

Of course, the semantics can be foggy. People use the word confidence more often than faith and I think they are closely related but I like "faith" more because faith is more humble than confidence.

Maybe this is because of the common usage of faith in "leap of faith" and how this seems to move the word into the realm of "belief in the face of the unknown"–or just belief when you can't have 100% certainty.

The Power of Faith

The power of faith is real power. Believing that you can attain your goal is of great importance for its achievement. Without faith, there will be doubts and disbelief, which lead to non-doing and to non-achievement.

When you have faith in a higher power, for me it is God, to help you, things start happening.

This power draws what you want into your life, whereas doubts, worries and disbelief push them away. (Faith and fear cannot occupy the same space at the same time; where faith is present fear leaves, where fear is present, faith leaves.)

If you read about the lives of people who have achieved success, you would discover that faith played a major role in their life.

These successful people believed that they could achieve their goals and had no doubts about it.

They visualized their goals as already achieved, as already a fact, and this is what you also need to do.

The power of faith and belief can change your life.

The faith I am talking about here, is the faith in yourself, and in the power of the God to manifest for you whatever you want.

It is the belief that you can achieve your goals.

It is the faith and belief that thoughts can turn into real things.

Faith in this sense, equals belief and certainty that what you want can come true. Faith strengthens the motivation to act and do things, and help you maintain the positive attitude necessary for success.

Faith is important, but alone it is not enough for success. You also need willpower, discipline and persistence. You also need to take positive action to show your faith.

Often, after reading a book, or attending a workshop about the powers of the mind or the law of attraction, people get excited about the potential within them. They feel thrilled, and believe that they can change their life.

However, too often, nothing happens, because interest and enthusiasm wane and so does faith.

In order to succeed, you have to keep alive the flame of desire, ambition and faith in oneself and in the ability to turn thoughts into reality.

Faith, feelings, desire and positive thinking are essential for achieving success, but so also positive action, persistence, willpower and self-discipline.

Attitude is important, but must reflect in actions. You should not just wait passively for things to happen.

Without faith, success in unattainable. You will not succeed if you do not have faith in your dreams, goals and yourself.

Faith encompasses a multitude of success characteristics: fortitude, persistence, mental stamina, grit, sticking it out during tough times, confidence, belief, conviction, certainty, hope, certainty, courage, tenacity, fearlessness, boldness, resoluteness, guts, intestinal fortitude, determination, resolve, will, willpower and toughness.

Faith means you never quit on your dreams, your goals and the pursuit of your main purpose in life. Those who have faith in their dreams, goals and their main purpose in life do not allow anything to get in their way. Faith enables you to overcome every obstacle in your path towards success.

Faith is the most important ingredient to success. With faith (God) all things are possible if you believe.

Why Having Faith is So Important

Sometimes, when things don't go according to plan, we lose faith, not only in ourselves, but also in any potential outcome in our lives. Failure will do that to you. When we experience life's monumental failures, it's easy to lose hope, and even faith.

But what's the difference?

Faith, at its core, is deep-rooted in the expectation of good things to come. It goes beyond hope. While hope lives in the mind, faith is steeped in the heart and the spirit. Faith can't be explained away by reason or logic, or be understood through a single dimension.

While life can be hard at the best of times, faith is the knowledge, deep down inside, that things will get better. It's taking the next step when you can't see the entire staircase. Simply put, life would fail to have reason if we didn't have faith.

We couldn't drive our cars without faith that someone wouldn't cross the divider and crash into us. If we didn't have faith, how could we fly in an airplane, a metalmachine soaring 35,000 feet in the air? Without faith, how could we move from one moment to the next without completely second-guessing every last thing that we did?

Without faith, we couldn't expect that things would turn out all right for us no matter what the situation might be.

Faith, then, is just as important as the air we breathe. While the oxygen in the air nourishes the body, faith nourishes the heart and the soul. It's the energy that courses through every single fiber and cell within our beings. It's part of every muscle and every strand of thought. It is the fundamental foundation of our existence.

Simply put, the importance of faith cannot be underestimated.

People have moved mountains with their faith. Even when situations seemed dire and bleak, it was their faith that carried them through. There's little to no explanation for it in the physical realm; it's the metaphysical fiber that binds us all, carrying each of our deepest wishes and desires. That's where faith lives.

Unfortunately, some people don't believe in things that they cannot see. They explain things away due to other causes and effects, failing to find the small miracles in life that exist and work in our favor on a constant basis. There's an enormous level of importance attributable to having faith in life.

5 Reasons to Have Faith

1. THE FOCUSED POWER OF FAITH BREEDS ABUNDANCE

The mind is an incredibly powerful tool. It can be used for good, but also go to waste when neglected or abused. In times of trouble, we tend to move away from positivity. We go from a state of abundance to a state of lack. But, faith is the tool that helps replenish abundance in the heart and the spirit, not just in the mind.

Whatever it is that we focus on in life, we get more of. If we focus on problems, we live solely in those problems and have difficulty moving past the negativity. Alternatively, however, when we focus on positivity and seek out solutions, we can resolve our problems and move from a state of lack back to a state of abundance.

When we train our minds to think in abundance, and we hold unwavering faith, we gravitate towards that. We attract good things because we believe and expect in good things to come. Similarly, when we believe and expect bad things to come, we also attract that into our lives.

Faith is the pathway for abundance, so be sure to hold it at the forefront of your mind. Don't be afraid to expect the very best for yourself. This isn't about being selfish or aimlessly wishing for things; this is about the true, utter, deep-down belief in your heart and your soul that things will improve, and that you deserve the very best in life.

2. WHAT DOESN'T KILL YOU MAKES YOU STRONGER

There's a powerful story in the Bible in the Book of Job. The story is about a man named Job who was as astute as any man could be. He believed strongly in God and held high in faith. But as the story goes, one day the devil paid God a visit. The topic of discussion? Job's faith.

The devil reasoned that Job was faithful because he had been blessed with so much in life. Family, money, land, and respect. The devil proposed that should God take any number of these things away from Job, he would no longer be the faithful man that God held him up to be. The devil claimed that Job would curse God and that his point would be all but proven. God, of course, disagreed.

So, this agreement began when God began taking things away from Job's life. Over the course of these trials, Job loses everything that he had worked so hard to create over the years. His livestock, all his money, his family, his friends, and his health. However, even when his wife told him he should curse God, Job didn't. He remained faithful.

Afterwards, God restored all of Job's worldly possessions, family, and health. To add to that, God multiplied what Job once had many times over. The moral of the story? Whatever doesn't kill you makes you stronger. Times might be bad and you might want to throw in that proverbial towel. But never lose faith. For a person without faith is likened to a stream without water — they would cease to exist.

3. FAITH HELPS YOU TO DISCOVER YOUR PURPOSE IN LIFE

Going through life and all of its ups and downs can take a toll on us. At times, it's enough to question our very existence. But through all of the trials and tribulations we might face, it's faith that gives us that helping hand. It works to guide us in the right direction, moving us towards and allowing us to discover our purpose in life.

This doesn't happen overnight. Usually, when we're faced with a difficult situation, it gets harder before it gets better. Little by little, a part of us is broken, until one day, we dig deep down inside and somehow find the strength we needed to make it through. That strength comes from our faith. Whether it's your faith in God or in something else, that faith shall set you free.

Everything in life is far easier to get through when we have faith. It's the guiding light that helps push us towards our purpose.

4. FAITH TRUMPS STRESS, ANXIETY, AND FEAR

It's easy to allow stress, anxiety, and fear to run our lives. We go from moment to moment worried about one thing or another. Sometimes, those worries manifest themselves into highly-stressful situations, causing not only mental anguish, but physical problems as well. There's a clear and documented connection between stress and the increased likelihood of disease and illness.

When we allow our minds to move into that realm unchecked, there's no telling of the damage that can be done,but it's faith that helps to keep those things at bay. Even when we have no reason to believe that things will get better, it's through faith that our situations do improve. When you hold the utter expectation of that in your mind, no challenge is too difficult.

Learn to harbor faith and use it to eliminate stress, anxiety, and fear. Think back to situations in the past when you made it through something you thought was insurmountable. Believe and expect that good things will happen, and they will. This isn't about ignoring your problems; this is about knowing that your situation will improve deep down inside your heart and your soul.

5. IT ACTS AS THE PATHWAY TO FINDING SOLUTIONS

Faith is the pathway to finding solutions in life. Keep in mind that human beings were made to thrive, and not just survive. If you're only surviving, there's far greater in store for you. There's a pathway to all of your solutions, and that pathway is steeped in faith and the expectation of greater things to come in time.

No matter what the situation is, no matter how bad or dire you think it might seem, your faith can and will get you through it. You must accept that as fact, and hold on to the expectation of greater things to come. Don't stop pushing or searching for an answer to help resolve whatever situation you might be facing in your life.

If you really want something in life, and I mean you really want it deep down inside and you have a strong-enough reason you absolutely must achieve it, faith is the thing that helps you to see that through. It's at the core of a persistent heart. Never give up on your hopes and your dreams just because you faced some initial setbacks. Lean on your faith as often as possible and you'll soon come to realize why having unwavering faith is so important in life.

3

FAVOUR

FAVOUR

The Secret of Extraordinary Success

Luke 2:52- "Jesus increased in wisdom and stature, and in favour with God and men."

Definition of Favour is, "An act of kindness beyond what is due or usual." It's when you get more than you deserve: I have worked hard, but not this hard. I have been good, but not that good. I have given, but not that much! Favour!

Favour is different than "Favours". Favours are often actions designed to influence, control, and manipulate others. This is a very different thing than Divine favour.

Favour is when others, out of good will, seek to benefit you. "He who earnestly seeks good finds favour" (Prov 11:25) Divine favour is when God pours out His benefits on you simply because your ways have pleased Him. (Ps 103:2) When a man's ways please the Lord He causes even your enemies to favour you! (Prov 16:7)

Six Ways To Grow In Favour With Both God And Man:

1. LIVE YOUR LIFE WHOLEHEARTEDLY FOR GOD.

"For You, O Lord, will bless the righteous: With favour You will surround him as with a shield." (Ps 5:12)

2. GOD IS REWARDER OF THOSE WHO DILIGENTLY SEEK HIM. (HEB11:6).

Was it an accident that Pharaoh showed favour to Joseph? Or that Daniel found favour with all of the kings he served under? No! They both diligently sought the Lord, even when it wasn't to their advantage. Do it!

3. PERSEVERANCE DURING THE PAIN OF CORRECTION, BRINGS LONG TERM FAVOUR.

"His anger is but for a moment, His favour is for life;" (Ps 30:5). "We count them blessed who endure. You have heard of the perseverance of Job and seen the end intended by the Lord-that the Lord is very compassionate and merciful." (James 5:11) Job kept the right heart attitude and received double for his trouble!

4. USE YOUR BUSINESS TO DO GOD'S BUSINESS, THEN GOD MAKES IT HIS BUSINESS TO BLESS YOUR BUSINESS!

"Let them shout for Joy and be glad who favour my righteous cause." (Ps 35:27) Peter lent his boat to Jesus and He blessed his business big time in return. (Luke 5:1-11) It takes a commitment to being involved in God's business if you want God's favour on your business.

5. ASK FOR FAVOUR FROM GOD AND MAN.

"You have not because you ask not." (Jam 4:2-3) Asking your boss for an increase at the right time and in the right way can cause favour to come your way. Try making a wise appeal like Queen Esther did. (Esther 5:1-8)

6. BLESSING OTHERS CAUSES YOU TO REAP FAVOUR WITH OTHERS.

Ruth finding favour with Boaz is a great example of this principle. (Ruth 2:2-13). God always has someone watching you who has the ability to bring you into your next season of blessing. Whenever possible, sow blessing into the lives of others.

Understanding the Place of Favour in Success

Success in life is a direct function of God's favour. Outstanding favour is what we call outstanding success; hence, favour is a fundamental requirement in the school of outstanding success. The dictionary defines favour as an act of kindness, something given as a token of love, affection, or remembrance. That is why Apostle Paul could boldly declare in 1 Corinthians 15:10: But by the grace of God I am what I am.... Favour delivers to us those things that by right don't belong to us but which God bring our way just to prove that we are in favour with Him. For instance, Joseph had favour with his father.

He was the only child Jacob made a coat of many colours for. His father favoured him so much that he became the envy of his brothers. Every outstanding accomplishment in life is traceable to the flow of favour. The Bible records: We have heard with our ears, O God, our fathers have told us, what work thou didst in their days, in the times of old. How thou didst drive out the heathen with thy hand, and plantedst them; how thou didst afflict the people, and cast them out. For they got not the land in possession by their own sword, neither did their own arm save them: but thy right hand, and thine arm, and the light of thy countenance, because thou hadst a favour unto them (Psalm 44:1-3).

Our blessings and liftings in life are all functions of God's favour. Jesus was an outstanding success while on earth here because He enjoyed God's favour which also brought about men's favour (Luke 2:40/52).

Stimulators of Divine Favour

There are certain things that provoke God's favour upon a man.

- **Knowledge:**

  We multiply grace (favour) through knowledge. As it is written: Grace and peace be multiplied unto you through the knowledge of God, and of Jesus our Lord (2 Peter 1:2). The way of the ignorant is hard (Proverbs 13:15). Knowledge multiplies favour while ignorance equals hardship. There is no mountain anywhere; every man's ignorance is his mountain. The Bible says: My son, eat thou honey, because it is good; and the honeycomb, which is sweet to thy taste: So shall the knowledge of wisdom be unto thy soul: when thou hast found it, then there shall be a reward, and thy expectation shall not be cut off (Proverbs 24:13-14). The knowledge of wisdom attracts rewards. We can't find the good Word of God and not attract favour. Wonderful favours are attracted by the knowledge of the truth.

- **Righteousness:**

  Righteousness causes us to enjoy favour first with God and then with men. The righteous has a heritage of favour with God. God compasses the righteous with favour. It is written: For thou, Lord, wilts bless the righteous; with favour wilt thou compass him as with a shield (Psalm 5:12). But, He is angry with the sinner every day. The Bible says: God judgeth the righteous, and God is angry with the wicked every day (Psalm 7:11). When we give in to sin, we step out of favour with God.

- **The Anointing of the Holy Spirit:**

  The anointing of the Holy Spirit carries supernatural favour. It naturally attracts favour to whomever or wherever it is found. When we are anointed with the Holy Spirit, we naturally smell of favour. It is written: Thou lovest righteousness, and hatest wickedness: therefore God, thy God, hath anointed thee with the oil of gladness above thy fellows. And the daughter of Tyre shall be there with a gift; even the rich among the people shall intreat thy favour (Psalm 45:7/12). Thus, the anointing of the Holy Spirit puts on us unction for divine enabling.

- **Kingdom Addiction:**

Kingdom addiction triggers divine favour. When we are addicted to the Kingdom of God, we compel favour to come our way. It is written: But seek ye first the kingdom of God, and his righteousness; and all these things shall be added unto you (Matthew 6:33; see also Psalm 102:13-14). We may ask, 'How do we favour His Kingdom?' We do by allowing whatever is done in the Kingdom touch us and letting whatever affects the Kingdom affect us.

10 Verses About Success

1. **Philippians 4:13** - I can do everything through him who gives me strength.
2. **Proverbs 16:3** - Commit to the Lord whatever you do, and your plans will succeed.
3. **Kings 2:3** - And observe what the Lord your God requires: Walk in his ways, and keep his decrees and commands, his laws and requirements, as written in the Law of Moses, so that you may prosper in all you do and wherever you go.
4. **Luke 16:10-11** - Whoever can be trusted with very little can also be trusted with much, and whoever is dishonest with very little will also be dishonest with much. So if you have not been trustworthy in handling worldly wealth, who will trust you with true riches?

5. **Isaiah 41:10** - So do not fear, for I am with you; do no be dismayed, for I am your God. I will strengthen and help you; I will uphold you with my righteous right hand.
6. **Jeremiah 17:7** - But blessed is the man who trusts in the Lord, whose confidence is in him.
7. **Deuteronomy 8:18** - But remember the Lord your God, for it is he who gives you the ability to produce wealth, and so confirms his covenant, which he swore to your forefathers, as it is today.
8. **Psalms 37:4**- Delight yourself in the Lord and he will give you the desires of your heart.
9. **Proverbs 3:1-4** - My son, do not forget my teaching, but let your heart keep my commandments, for length of days and years of life and peace they will add to you. Let not steadfast love and faithfulness forsake you; bind them around your neck; write them on the tablet of your heart. So you will find favor and good success in the sight of God and man.
10. **James 4:10** - Humble yourselves before the Lord, and he will exalt you.

4

PASSION

PASSION

Follow Your Passions, and Success Will Follow

Whether an individual is considering starting a small business or changing career paths, it is important that passion is factored into the equation. While characteristics such as strong values, talent, ambition, intellect, discipline, persistence, and luck all contribute to business and career success, following your passion can often make the biggest difference of all.

The True Meaning of Success

Before discussing passion and explaining its significance, we must first define the true meaning of success. Success is usually thought of as making large sums of money or achieving a certain level of fame, but true success that satisfies is not all about money.

Success is better defined as an achievement of a desired aim or purpose. More than money or fame, most people desire to align their own passions with their work, while making a sustainable income.

Money brings diminishing returns the more you make, which makes it an elusive definition of success.

For most people, success means being proud of their achievements and being part of something that matters. This is particularly true when it comes to meaningful work. In fact, if an individual decides to follow their passion, there is a greater likelihood that money and traditional success will follow, because the time and effort invested in the venture come with enthusiasm and zeal.

Follow Your Passion and Succeed: 4 Icons Who Did

1. **Steve Jobs**

    One of the most successful companies in the world is **Apple**. Apple's founder and most notable leader was the late Steve Jobs. In an article titled, "The Seven Success Principles of Steve Jobs," writer Carmine Gallo outlines seven factors responsible for Jobs' success. The article is based on interviews with Apple employees and Steve Jobs himself. The first principle? "Do what you love." Steve Jobs believed in the power of passion and once said, "People with passion can change the world for the better." Jobs claimed that the passion he had for his work made all the difference.

2. **Chris Gardner**

    Chris Gardner, the once homeless man turned multi-millionaire stockbroker and featured in the movie The Pursuit of Happiness expressed what he believes is the secret to success. According to Gardner, the secret is to "find something you love to do so much you can't wait for the sun to rise to do it all over again." He explains that the most inspiring leaders are those who do not simply work but pursue a calling.

3. **Mark Zuckerberg**

    Facebook's CEO, Mark Zuckerberg, has changed the world in which we live. In David Kirkpatrick's book The Facebook Effect:

The Inside Story of the Company That is Connecting The World, Kirkpatrick lists what he believes are Zuckerberg's characteristics that led to his success.

One of these characteristics is following his passion, not money. Zuckerberg suggests "following your happiness" when at a crossroads, using the logic that even if you do not end up making a fortune, you will at least be doing what you love.

4. **Warren Buffett** Warren Buffett, known as "the Oracle of Omaha," is probably one of the greatest investors of all time. But even Buffett knows there is more to success than money. In an interview with Parade Magazine, Buffett outlined ten ways to get rich. He concluded his list of advice with, "Know what success really means." He explains the importance of finding what it is that brings true meaning and what makes each day important. This should be the focus of an individual's efforts.

Why Passion Matters

Among the traits and abilities that lead to success, passion stands alone. Unlike skill, knowledge, or other factors, passion is innate: it can't be learned or acquired but is always present. Passion, an overwhelming drive to reach one's goals, is the one factor that unites all successful people in equal measure.

Passion powers the hard work, determination, and creativity that make great accomplishments possible. Successful novelists, film directors, scientists, CEOs, world-class athletes, and other people who have risen to the tops of their fields all possess a deep motivation that gives them the wherewithal to work extraordinarily hard at something even when it's uncertain how, when, and even if they will enjoy rewards for their efforts.

Because passion can't be taught or faked, recruiters need to be able to identify truly passionate candidates reliably. This is no easy task, especially because people who are passionate about getting a job may not necessarily be passionate about doing that job once they have it. But the ability to identify genuine passion is critical to being able to hire the best possible candidates.

Failure As A Precursor To Success

The etymology of the word passion is the Latin pati, which means "to suffer" or "to endure." Over the centuries, the meaning of passion has evolved considerably. But one enduring aspect is the idea that it involves a certain degree of **forbearance**.

Work is rarely easy. Succeeding at work requires a willingness to grit one's teeth, dig deep, and grind it out when the going gets tough. It also means not quitting when something doesn't work out as intended or hoped. Passion can help people power over these hurdles— another reason why it is a desirable trait among successful candidates.

Regardless of a person's industry, career path, or talent level, he or she will inevitably encounter some failure and might not achieve success for years. The path to success looks more like a zigzag than a straight line. How well a candidate is prepared to endure, learn from, and overcome setbacks will determine his or her performance. For example, Steffi Graf played on the professional tennis circuit for almost five seasons before winning the first of her 22 Grand Slam titles—a feat she probably would not have accomplished if she had reacted badly to losing!

Identifying how candidates respond to failure is essential to identifying their resilience. People who deal with failure by assessing and adapting are apt to see it as an opportunity to learn and improve. But responding positively to failure is impossible for people who don't care enough about why they're doing what they're doing in the first place. **Passion is what generates the desire to learn, try again, and do better next time.**

WHY PASSION IS IMPORTANT FOR SUCCESS

I bet you have heard it a gazillion time that you need to have passion for what you do to be successful. But, have you ever thought about why is passion so important for success?

I have been in the personal development industry for over a decade, and I'm telling you that passion is one of the keys to success.

Yes, passion may not guarantee your success, but it can greatly increase and boost your chances of what you pursue in life.

And in this book, I'm going to share with you 7 reasons why you need to have the passion in order to be successful in life. Here are the 7 reasons...

1. **Passion fuels your motivation**

    First, passion fuels your motivation. Often times, people fail to achieve the success they desire because they lack the motivation. In the beginning, they are so motivated with their newly set goals. Most people are driven in the early phase when they first started a project.

    But after a while, when they don't get the results they want, or when they don't see any returns that they have expected, they started to lose steam.

    People will start to lose interest in their project/goal when they fail to produce any significant success from their hard work.

    Not to mention all the distractions and hustle-bustle of daily life. When you started to lose your drive, you will put in less effort, which leads to fewer results.

    And this is why most people give up in the end. They fail to sustain their motivation over the long-term.

    You have to understand that success is not a sprint, but a marathon. And because of this, you need to learn how to build sustainable motivation to support your action.

    And having a passion for what you do is one of the best ways to maintain your motivation.

    This is why when you are passionate about what you do; you

tend to be able to stay motivated for a longer period, which increases your chances of success.

2. **Passion boots your focus**

   Have you heard about the phrase called "**flow state**"? When you are in the right mood of doing something, you enter the flow state and you become so focused that you become fully immersed in the work.

   When you are passionate about the things that you do, it is easier for you to enter the flow state.

   For instance, I use to love to play basketball. There were many times when I've been in the game, I enter into the flow state. I became so immersed in the game that my body reacts automatically to the shot.

   Within split seconds, I know what to do, how to take the shot and how to react on a made basket then return to defense. I become fully focused and energized. There will be no distractions because the game is all that matters.

   This is what happens when you are passionate about what you do.

   If you want to achieve great success in life, you must experience more flows. This is why you want to pursue your passion because the more passionate you are with what you do, the easier you can enter the flow state.

   And the more flow you experience, the better your work quality. It helps you focus and produces greater achievement in life.

3. **Passion allows you to be more creative**

   Think about it, if you don't like to do a particular thing, will you become creative with it? The answer is obvious, isn't it?

   On the other hand, if you are passionate about something, do you think you will become creative and good at it? Again, you know the answer.

   When you are passionate about something, you will become creative with it. You will want to produce greater results doing it because you love to do it.

However, if you hate doing something, all you think about will be how to quickly get it done or how NOT to do it.

Your focus is different. When you are passionate about gaming, you focus on how you can win the game beautifully. But when you are NOT passionate about games, probably, you will only play it to kill time. You don't care about the results or progress; you play it because you are bored.

Can you see the difference right now?

When someone is passionate with what he does, he will do it with his full heart. He will focus, be more creative, and enjoy the work.

On the contrary, when he is doing something that he dislikes, he will never enjoy it and he will want to get the work done as soon. He probably doesn't care about the results let alone the progress.

This is why passion is important for your success.

4. **Passion makes you happier**

   Let me ask you this simple question – do you prefer to do something you are passionate about or something that you dislike doing?

   Of course, you will go for the first option. And when you are doing something that you love, you become happier and more fulfilled.

   When you are happy and fulfilled, you tend to deliver a better job.

   You don't complain about work. You don't blame others when things go wrong. You will even volunteer yourself for the work. This is what makes the difference between having the passion and without it.

5. **Passion attracts other passionate people**

Do you want to work with people who are boring and who dislike their job? Or do you prefer to work with/for people who are passionate about their work?

Think about extraordinary people like Steve Jobs, Elon Musk, Bill Gates, Warren Buffett, Michael Jordan, Lionel Messi, and actors like Dwayne Johnson. These are people who are absolutely passionate about their work.

They love what they do, and because of their passion, they managed to attract a huge following and fans around the world. People admire them and people want to work with or for them.

Therefore, passion can help you attract other passionate people.

If you lack the passion for what you do, people can notice it and feel it. They know that you are doing your work because of the pay. You're not doing it for the passion.

Ask yourself;

- do you want to work with people who are passionate about what they do
- do you prefer to work with people who are only doing the work for the sake of it?

If you are a leader of a company, do you want to hire passionate people or people who only work for their salary? The answer is clear.

Like attracts like. And your passion can attract other passionate people to you too.

This is why successful people have and make friends with other successful people. This is one of the most important keys to success.

6. YOU WILL HAVE LESS STRESS

Stress is a major issue these days. People are stressed because of their work, personal lives, health, etc.

Iif you want to do better in life and achieve greater success, you must learn to have the passion not just in what you do, but in other areas of your life as well.

Imagine having a relationship where you don't have the passion. Can this relationship survive or thrive?

The same goes for every area of your life. You must develop passion for what you do and in every area of your life. When you are passionate about life and everything you do, you will experience less stress.

You don't look at problems as problems. Instead, you will treat problems as challenges and you love them.

As a result, you become more successful than most ordinary people. Do you know why passion is important now?

7. PASSION EQUIPS YOU WITH POSITIVE ATTITUDES

Finally, passion can equip you with positive attitudes.

When you are passionate with what you do, you will never give up.

Successful people love what they do, and that is why they don't mind to fail and then start over again. They simply love what they do that they care more about the progress than the result.

When you are passionate with what you do, you will become an optimist.

You will strive for improvement. You will want to do better. You will not give up and you will have stronger determination. Most importantly, you will become positive and believe that things will work out for you as long as you work on it.

This is how extraordinary people make it. They are passionate with what they do,and this is why they are successful.

Make Your Dreams Real: How to Find Your Passion in Life

Living well means more than just having essential needs met. Deep down, we all strive for meaning beyond the bare necessities. Even if you appear successful, you can still feel like something is missing, and you continue to wonder how to find your passion in life.

Each person has a heart dream, a unique drive to make a contribution and fulfill a purpose. Discovering your passion, and dedicating yourself to pursuing it, can make a big difference in your happiness, self-motivation, and achievement.

When all the pieces fit together, combining your passion with your strengths, you can achieve things you never imagined. It is entirely possible to reinvent yourself, even changing careers at any age.

Most people don't start out knowing what they want to be when they grow up. And those that do often discover later in life they made the wrong choice. It's not uncommon to become completely disengaged from what your younger self was sure was a true calling.

In my coaching practice, I speak with people every day who are seeking change. They are looking for a new challenge to bring the spark of passion back into their lives. I've developed some tools that help people navigate this winding path, discover passions, and take action to develop them into meaningful passion projects, businesses, or new careers.

When you can't quite figure out how to discover your passion, these actionable strategies will help you begin. You'll also learn some new ways to think about how passion can fit into your life and how to sustain it through the inevitable challenges.

1. MAKE A LIST OF 100 ASPIRATIONS

Do you come up with a complete blank when you ask yourself, "What is my passion?" Or, do you have so many interests swirling around your brain, that you couldn't possibly choose one?

Either way, brainstorming can help you get a sense of direction — it will provide a big list of clues on where to start looking. It will also open you up to exciting ideas and spark the courage to begin exploring them.

I suggest spending some time to get all your ideas out of your head and onto a page.

This is a brainstorming exercise, but it's more than that. Making a list of 100 Aspirations tapping into the power of self-expression and creativity. According to neuroscience, expressing your heart dreams, without fear of judgment or limited thinking, is a powerful way to create possibilities for growth and connection.

Dedicate a week to brainstorm your potential passions. Spend time every day writing down projects, activities, causes, creative outlets, or potential career paths that you'd love to go after. As you revisit your list throughout the week, you may feel inspired to come up with new ideas.

As you brainstorm on how to find what you're passionate about, it can be tough to get past the blank page. Start with these questions:

- If there was a dream job, what would it be for you?
- What adventures and activities intrigue you?
- If you could make the impossible happen, what would you want?
- What sparks your curiosity?
- If you had all the resources available, and you know you wouldn't fail, what would you want to happen?

After about a week of building your list, you may already feel motivated to make a shift toward pursuing one of your passions. Do you notice any hobbies or interests on your list of aspirations that you'd like to spend more time doing? You can add passion to your life right away by setting aside more time to explore those pursuits.

Choosing what to do for a living can simply be a means of enjoying your life. That is a legitimate way to treat your passion. Don't think that work has to be the only outlet.

However, you may notice some ideas from your list to help guide you towards a career you can be passionate about. For example, if you consider yourself a crime TV junkie, perhaps consider a career in criminal justice or law enforcement.

Remember that pursuing a passion might not always mean changing careers. Your greatest passion doesn't have to be the thing that keeps a roof over your head. You may find meaning in your life outside of the office, perhaps by supporting a social cause, spending more time with friends and family, or focusing on a hobby.

2. TALK ABOUT YOUR POTENTIAL PASSIONS

It's not enough to make a list and dream about pursuing a potential passion. Finding what you are truly passionate about will involve some fear, uncertainty, and risk.

One of the best ways to start getting more comfortable with those feelings is to start talking about your dreams.

From your list of 100 aspirations, choose a few of the most exciting items, the ones that are a little bit scary. Find a supportive, non-judgmental friend or colleague to share these with. Ask them to simply listen and discuss what these heart dreams mean to you.

When you talk about your aspirations at this stage, make sure you choose the right person. What you don't want is criticism or reasons you can't or shouldn't pursue these dreams. The goal right now is only to experience what it feels like to speak your heart dreams out loud, to yourself and someone you trust.

Here are some questions your conversation partner can ask you, to make this process more meaningful:

- What is important to you about this aspiration?
- How long have you had this aspiration?
- What do you like the most about this aspiration?

3. FOCUS ON ONE GOAL (NOT A DREAM)

You may have a ton of ideas on what you might be passionate about. Chasing after too many passions will make it difficult to find enough time to see results. To make real change, you'll need to learn how to prioritize your life around your most important goals.

When you made your list of aspirations and started talking about some of your passions, this was a creative, heart-centered exercise, but making a big change requires planning and action. You have to switch to a more goal-oriented approach, using a different part of the brain, to bring your passion to the forefront of your life.

I suggest narrowing down your direction, and choosing one of your aspirations to transform into a concrete goal. That means setting a date to start, and a date when you will reach that goal.

4. EXPRESS YOURSELF CREATIVELY

If you still feel stuck in discovering your passion, I suggest participating in creative activities. Expressing yourself creatively will help take brainstorming a step further, and make new connections in your mind.

Research suggests that things like expressive writing, dance, visual arts therapy, and music can help relieve stress and process life events. You'll open your mind to make new connections and encourage your brain to find new ways to answer, "What is my passion?"

Don't be afraid to return to a passion that has sat dormant. Sometimes revisiting an old hobby or interest years later, you'll find renewed passion and fulfillment.

5. CREATE A VISION STATEMENT

Visualization is a powerful technique. Studies show that imagining yourself achieving something actually improves your chances of success.

Think of visualization as a bio-hack to actualize your passion and achieve your best. You use this technique by creating a vision statement that outlines the current and future goals you have in mind:

- Write down "why" this passion matters to you.
- Explain some of the steps that it will take to pursue this passion.
- Visualize yourself completing those steps.

Alternatively, you can create a vision board. Take a poster board or bulletin board. Cut out magazine clippings and create a collage of your goals. They can include words, phrases, or pictures that relate to your passion.

Keep your vision board in an area of the house or office where you will see it each day. This will remind you to spend time visualizing your goals daily.

6. SET SMALL GOALS

Passion requires action to yield results.

When you recognize those big heart dreams, you know which direction you need to go. But passion, without action, won't lead you forward. Sometimes, we feel the passion drain out of a project when we fail to achieve what we set out to do, or it takes too long to see results.

That's why it's crucial to figure out the steps you need to take to accomplish your goals.

Neuroscientists have discovered a great bio-hack to help. Research has found that your brain releases a feel-good neurotransmitter called dopamine each time you complete a task. (Have you ever noticed how satisfying it feels to check an item off a to-do list?)

You set yourself up for success by breaking down a big goal into smaller tasks. Each time you complete a step, you'll feel good and motivated to keep going. Building this self-motivation into the process will help you continue to pursue your passion, even when it gets hard.

Create a "passion to-do list." Ask yourself:

- What do you want to accomplish with your passion?
- What small steps will it take to achieve that dream?

Break down your goal into small steps. Then schedule a timeline to complete each goal. Give yourself enough space and flexibility for you to attend to them.

7. DEVOTE TIME TO YOUR PASSION EACH DAY

Consistent effort to pursue your passion will turn your dream life into a reality.

Set aside a chunk of time each day to work toward your passion. That might mean 30 minutes of practicing guitar in the evening, or applying to one job in your dream career every day.

Daily planning can help devote time to your passion and stick to it long enough to see results.

8. CREATING HABITS FOR SUCCESS

They don't get stuck daydreaming about what they want to achieve. Instead, they take actionable strategies toward moving forward with their passion projects, such as:

- Setting small goals and completing them, one step at a time
- Creating positive environments, surrounded by supportive people who encourage them to pursue their passions
- Recognizing opportunities and seizing them, rather than turning them down
- Accepting mistakes because they are part of the learning process
- Focusing on how to move forward, instead of dwelling on previous failures
- Holding themselves accountable on what they can control, rather than blaming others

9. EXPLORE, EXPERIMENT, EVALUATE

The pathway to your passion may not be straightforward. It's most often a winding path leading to new discoveries.

As you explore different avenues, you may run into dead-ends, twists, and turns. Think of it as a learning experience that guides you from where you are now to where you want to be.

Go into it with an open mind, a mindset of experimentation. It's possible that you have not yet encountered that thing you really want to do — maybe you haven't heard of it, or it hasn't yet been discovered or invented. Keep an eye out.

Writing in a journal will help you reflect on your experience and tune in to the right path. You may realize something you thought you loved doesn't really make you happy. Learn to walk away.

Sometimes we don't know what we want until we see other people doing something that speak to us. So get out there and witness the world and what other folks are doing.

10. EMBRACE UNCERTAINTY

The pursuit of a passion requires hard work, dedication, and a willingness to fail.

Actually, the root of the word comes from "**to suffer.**" Results don't happen overnight. As any successful entrepreneur, CEO, or artist will tell you, pursuing their passion comes with a lot of hard work. They didn't just wake up one day and achieve it all. It takes a suffering of sorts, a grit and mental toughness to fail, get up, and fail again, to keep on trying.

When you learn to embrace change, you can better manage those feelings of discomfort.

Some passionate folks set out to accomplish something because they have a strong desire and a strong draw toward a goal or dream. However, when things get hard, and you have to dig in, passion may give way to grit and determination. That's okay.

11. GET AN ACCOUNTABILITY PARTNER

Studies show that sharing your goals with a friend will improve your chances of succeeding. Look for someone who can support you without judgment.

If you don't have anyone in your circle, you can join groups and forums online, or even set up a more formal mastermind group of people who have a similar goal or passion.

This support system is crucial to staying motivated, refocusing when you get off track, and making steady progress. Together, you can brainstorm how to navigate obstacles and celebrate achievements.

This social support works best when you can schedule regular check-ins with your accountability partners. Build it into your schedule to make sure it happens regularly.

12. SPEAK WITH A COACH OR MENTOR

Research confirmed the positive outcomes of having a mentor or coach. In the workplace, those with a mentor benefit from improved ability to work on a team, higher work satisfaction, and better job performance.

As you work to develop a new passion, whether it's a career goal or a personal hobby, a mentor can guide you with the benefit of their experience. They've already faced the challenges you're facing now, and you can learn from how they moved forward.

If you don't have access to mentorship in the field of your new passion, consider reaching out to a coach. Skilled business coaches can help you chart a path through work and business transitions. We can also help you find out why you're feeling uninspired with your career and get back the sense of passion you're missing.

If you're struggling to navigate a major change, scheduling a meeting with a coach is one of the most helpful gifts you can give yourself.

13. CELEBRATE EVERY SMALL WIN

When you work hard toward a passion, you deserve to celebrate. Celebrating achievements will boost your confidence and help to stay motivated.

Small wins can be tiny, but still worth celebrating. For example:

- Sticking to your plan to explore a new hobby this weekend, or renew an old one.
- Trying something new, and realizing you don't love it — that's a step towards finding what you do love.
- Spending an hour researching online classes to learn more about a potential passion.

Check-in with your coach, mentor, or accountability partners to remind yourself that you are making progress, no matter how small. When you reach a step you are proud of, celebrate with loved ones or make a point of rewarding yourself and doing something you enjoy.

5

RESILIENCE

RESILIENCE

Resilience: The Key To Success

In psychology, resilience is an individual's tendency to cope with stress and adversity. This coping may result in the individual "bouncing back" to a previous state of normal functioning, or simply not showing negative effects.

The training and education you receive in school might help you attain the skills required to actually do your job, but there is more to success than that. These days, it's soft skills that set you apart from the pack. Traits like excellent communication, the ability to work well in a team, and professional resiliency go a long way. Resiliency may not be discussed quite as much as some of the other skills, but it's very important. So, what does it mean to be resilient in a professional context? How can resiliency change your career.

1. RESILIENCE MEANS ADAPTABILITY AND EMOTIONAL STRENGTH.

Resilience is all about how well you're able to adjust to changes in the world around you. In a professional context, resiliency allows you to roll with the punches with greater ease. On difficult days, when others might push back against the tides of change, or get hung up on defeats, resilient people differentiate themselves as leaders. They adapt quickly to changes on an emotional level, not just a practical one, and that sets them apart.

Focus on cultivating some of the characteristics of resilient professionals, like confidence, optimism, and compassion, in order to help you move further down this path. Even just understanding the goal itself could make a big difference. When you appreciate the impact that resiliency could have on your professional life, it becomes a priority. And, that helps you further develop and hone the trait.

2. IT HELPS YOU BOUNCE BACK QUICKLY.

Resilience isn't about accepting defeat; it's about springing back from it easily and quickly. When you believe in your work, and yourself, and when you're able to see challenges as opportunities, everything starts to change. Our professional lives are full of disappointments, great and small. Being able to quickly bounce back from them could help you advance your career in countless ways.

3. YOU'LL ADJUST WELL TO CHANGES.

Our world changes so quickly these days. If you're the kind of worker who's going to hem-and-haw every time the company updates the way they're doing things, you're going to fall behind. Resiliency helps you to adjust well to changes, which helps you to become a valued asset around the office. You'll be known as someone who adapts well, and someone who helps others to do the same via your example.

4. RESILIENCE IS INFECTIOUS.

When one person offers this kind of perspective, they become invaluable within a group — certainly in an employer's eyes. Negative coworkers are a drag, but, resilient people have a way of putting a positive, lighthearted spin on things. It's hard to maintain a dreary attitude when sitting next to someone with a resilient spirit, because the contrast makes the negativity stand out even more than usual. Be the kind of employee who influences others in a positive direction. Your employer will notice the impact you're having on the collective culture of your workplace.

5. YOU'LL FEEL BETTER.

Cultivating more resiliencies isn't just about getting ahead at work — it's about being happier and healthier too. Resilience helps you reduce stress. This trait is really all about staying grounded and managing adversity. When you're better able to accept setbacks, recover quickly from disappointments, and adapt well to change, you deal with stress better. Resilience is the key to success because it changes your attitude and the way you respond to difficulty. Not only can it help you advance professionally, you'll also feel better and enjoy the ride a little more too.

Resilience - The fundamental Building Block of Success

According to my experience the primary difference between winners and losers is how they handle setbacks and how they cope with losing. Without a doubt, even the strongest, cleverest, and most competent ones among us stumble from time to time and do not succeed. Some of these challenges might be relatively minor. Others might be much larger in scale.

The real skill, and as such the main building block of success, is getting back on track again after difficult experiences and loses, and not giving up. Instead bouncing back into the original, or even into a stronger position than before.

Resilience, however, is not a silver bullet which automatically eliminates all problems of someone. It gives people the strength to directly face problems, to overcome adversity and to move on with their lives. (e.g. after a personal loss, sickness, nature catastrophe, etc.). People are able to marshal the strength to not just survive, but to prosper.

Start Developing Your Resilience Today

Developing your resilience will help you cope with stress and changes at work and lead by example. This will make you a sought-after leader in your field, and someone who earns the praise and respect of your team and peers.

Ten Ways to become more resilient

There are people who naturally possess certain personality traits that assist them coping with setbacks and bringing them quickly back on a good track. Today we know that many of these skills can be learned and trained by anyone. As such they will help you to tackle past or upcoming problems head-on and to become more successful.

1. UNDERSTAND THAT SETBACKS ARE PART OF LIFE

Life is not always cozy and fun. It is also characterized by complexity and challenges. They belong to life like the night is part of the day. Without night there would be no day. Without pain there would be no joy. While we often cannot avoid all the problems, we can choose to stay flexible, open-minded, and determined to succeed.

2. BE AWARE OF YOURSELF AND THE ENVIRONMENT

Resilient people are aware of themselves, the environment, and their own emotional reactions to those around them. They have understood the importance of evaluating the reasons of their feelings by constantly observing themselves. This enables them to take control of the situation and to develop various options of behaving and acting.

3. BELIEVE AND KNOW THAT YOU ARE IN CONTROL

If you are a resilient person, then you have a so-called Internal Locus of Control. You believe that you can control your life, you do not believe that you are defined by external factors which you can t control. Instead, you feel that you have the power to make choices and take actions that will affect your success rate.

4. BECOME A SOLUTION THINKER

When a difficult situation arises, resilient people would always think of solutions. They would act calmly, would review holistically the task at hand, and would be able to spot possible solutions. If not, they would envision them. Next time you encounter a new challenge, make a quick list of some of the potential ways you could solve it. Experiment with different strategies and focus on developing a logical way to work through it.

5. BELIEVE IN YOURSELF

You are unique. You are beautiful. You have proven already so often in life that you are an achiever. Remind yourself of your strengths and accomplishments. Believe in yourself and become more confident about your own abilities and strengths.

6. SET GOALS AND DEFINE MANAGEABLE MILESTONES

Difficult situations can be extremely daunting. Resilient people are able to view these situations in a realistic way, and then set reasonable goals to deal with the problem. When you find yourself becoming overwhelmed by a situation, take a step back to simply assess what is before you. Brainstorm possible solutions, and then break them down into manageable steps. Be willing to adapt, if necessary. Remain flexible and embrace change.

7. STAY OPTIMISTIC

Keeping a hopeful attitude during turbulent times is another key part of resilience. This does not mean ignoring problems at hand in order to focus on positive outcomes. It means understanding that setbacks are transient and that you have the skills and abilities to combat the challenges you face. What you are dealing with may be difficult, but it is important to remain hopeful and positive about a brighter future. View yourself as winner, not as a loser.

8. BE BRAVE AND ASK FOR HELP

Resilient people are mature enough to admit that they can t know everything. They are also strong enough to admit, if they feel that their energy level is going down and that they need to re-charge their batteries by receiving outside know-how, advice, support, etc. from any potential source of assistance. In this respect it helps if you have a good social network. If you can exchange with family, friends, or colleagues in order to gain new perspectives and/ or motivation.

9. TAKE IT EASY

Even the best among us will not be able to achieve everything. Even if they are properly prepared, have done their homework, can rely on an excellent support network, are super optimistic, and absolutely committed, there are still factors outside of our control. And, most importantly, often things just need time to evolve and to develop. Resilient people understand that sometimes the best recipe of success is to step back and to wait. They know that patience often pays off. They do not get stressed out in such situations. Rather they relax, re-focus on themselves and getting ready for possible next steps.

10. NURTURE YOURSELF

When you're stressed, it can be all too easy to neglect your own needs. Losing your appetite, ignoring exercise, and not getting enough sleep are all common reactions to a crisis situation. Focus on building your self-nurture skills, even when you are troubled. Make time for activities that you enjoy. By taking care of your own needs, you can boost your overall health and resilience and be fully ready to face life's challenges.

Now, tell me what do you think?

- What is your opinion about resilience?
- What is your recipe of success?
- What do you think is the ultimate characteristic of successful people?

6

REJUVENATION

REJUVENATION

Rejuvenating Your Business!!

Rejuvenation often brings to mind plastic surgery. As a verb, to rejuvenate means 'to become young again, to return to life or give new life or energy and to develop new youthful features'. Perhaps it is time to do a little plastic surgery on your business.

The root word for rejuvenate is "juvenile". Juveniles are young children who act and play without the cares of the world. They take chances as they haven't faced fears at this point of their lives. If they have fears, it's because their parents put them there.

What fears have been implanted into your business? In order to rejuvenate a company, something new always has to be in the works. In order to keep a company fresh a new product, marketing campaign or sales technique is constantly being introduced. Microsoft or Apple keeps advancing their businesses by creating new innovations on a regular basis. For sales professionals everyday must be exciting and greeted as if a child waiting for Christmas.

No matter what is happening in the economy, creating a challenging and exciting vision for you will make each day a new adventure. What do you want your income to be? What will you need to do to make that happen? What will you need to do different to make it happen? It has been said that to do the same thing over and over and expect different results is a definition of insanity. Stop the insanity!

Focus is everything. Focus on what you want and it will come into your lives. Simplify your business. As a kid, there weren't any cares to worry about. As an adult, there is consistently a full plate of cares and concerns. The benefit of having a business plan, having a vision for your business and for your life is that it allows you to simplify. You can weed out, delegate, and eliminate all activities that don't contribute to your goals that you have set for yourself. Everyday offers the opportunity for hidden treasures.

Remember the fun of an old-fashion scavenger hunt? The excitement of the clues, hunting for the treasures, and the satisfaction of finally finding the elusive prize. Let that enthusiasm seep into your daily hunt for business. Each new prospect or opportunity is a new prize and prospecting is the number one activity for your business to stay healthy.

Create daily goals and reward yourself when you are successful. Look for opportunities that you haven't tried before. Break the old routines and establish new ones. Toss out the old ways that you've done business and start new ones. By making these changes in your business, you will start to feel as you did when you got into the business. Change is good and new opportunities will come from your efforts.

Remember, it is profoundly significant that the only thing over which you have complete control is your own mental attitude. Find the master key. You'll find it when you're ready to seek. It's there waiting for you. Education is at your fingertips. Utilize your time to the fullest advantage. Quit listening to sports and talk radio. Stop spending your drive time to return phone calls. Get books on tape and listen to new ideas how to improve yourself and your business. Shut off the TV at 8 or 9PM and read for an hour. If you did that daily, you will read a book a week or 52 books a year. Just think of the knowledge you will gain from this simple act.

The easiest of is choosing happy and motivated people to hang out with. You know those who brighten a room when they leave it. Find young and upcoming people who don't know about defeat. It's amazing how they will up the level of excitement and energy in your office. Even with decades of experience, you will learn much about selling to the X and Y generation. Don't discount the young, sometimes what they bring to the table will more than compensate for their lack of experience. Find motivated and happy people and hang out with them. It will rejuvenate your office, your business and your attitude.

Business rejuvenation is too important to leave until it's essential

When a business falls on hard times, the choice is simple: spark the process of rejuvenation or risk losing everything.

Rejuvenation means restoring business health, not just avoiding total failure. It means taking a genuine 'thinking outside the box' approach, a heavy injection of fresh perspective and almost always a change in organizational culture. But should this really be limited to companies that are facing the sound of their own death knell?

Anyone responsible for a thriving enterprise knows that businesses, like bodies, face the prospect of ultimate failure from the very day they are created. The outside environment changes, new threats and opportunities emerge; and the internal organization gradually succumbs to a kind of corporate arteriosclerosis.

The business that does not adapt to the changes around it and the slow changes within it will ultimately fail.

The management approach to corporate turnaround is the very same approach that will keep a healthy business thriving. It is also the right approach to a successful start-up. What is it?

The ingredients of business failure can be engrained in company culture

"Match the Hatch" is the formula for a fly fisherman who wants success. It means being in the right place at the right time, with the right tackle, the right bait and with the best technique.

To succeed companies have to do the same.

To give a start up the best chance of success you must match the strategy, team, product and route to market as near as you can to the ideal. The same is true for already successful businesses. Companies must adapt to reality, whether at the beginning of their corporate lives or continuously during the high noon of their success. Unfortunately. many do not.

The DNA of an organization, particularly at management level, often plays a huge role in any corporate failure and certainly in start-up success. In established businesses, there is a natural tendency to adhere to the original formula that created the success, but which is increasingly not matching the need.

This adherence is often reinforced by falling into the trap of repeatedly recruiting and promoting those the top managers perceive to be like themselves. It reinforces entrenched attitudes and closes off adaptation to new opportunities and emerging threats. Diversity may be awkward to manage, but it is a guard against complacency.

Refusal to accept the situation

It's a strange reality of the corporate world that it's much more difficult to run a successful business than one that's in trouble. In a business that's deemed to be successful, it can be too easy to operate in blissful ignorance of potential external threats and internal inherent weaknesses until it is too late. Those that do highlight issues can simply be dismissed as negative, or causing unnecessary problems, and the issues flagged become the proverbial elephant in the room.

Perhaps a little paranoia by the CEO at the height of success might have guarded against such hubris. In my experience as a turnaround specialist, it was often only necessary to simply highlight the latent issues to which the overall organisation had averted its eyes; most people knew they were there and what to do about them, they just didn't like to appear disloyal.

Failing situations present opportunities to the right individuals

At the outset the temptation is to be prescriptive, but the best approach is to ask key stakeholders what they thought the answers were, but only after providing a point of reflection for them to self identify the issues. It is hard to do that in an apparently successful business, but when a business is on a near-fatal slide, often many of those that had refused to acknowledge a problem depart the stage.

For those that wanted rejuvenation this is the most exciting time, because the stage has been cleared of obstacles. Suddenly the space is available to tackle the challenge without distraction or the risk of it being hijacked.

Typically after around nine months, as the business starts to emerge from peril, those individuals who got in the way of admitting problems will begin to re-emerge, often having forgotten nothing and learning little from the experience. It seems obvious that a successful corporate turnaround will require a fundamental change in the culture of the organization to guard against a relapse.

Employing a continuous process of self-reflection and repositioning of your culture and business conventions will keep things permanently fresh. In an ideal world, companies should regularly rotate staff, promote young talent, weed out underperformance, change organisational structure to avoid stale thinking and review standard processes.

Major new products or market initiatives are often seen as a threat to those charged with the management of the existing order. The antidote is to cherry pick the best talent available from all parts of the organisation and set up the new division outside existing structures to avoid the natural temptation of those who feel threatened by the new initiative to stifle it at birth.

Corporate turnaround as a continual process

Seeing things as they are is a key component of success in any enterprise, be it start-up, successful business or one that is failing. Businesses need to be able to anticipate changes on the horizon.

It's a reluctance to recognize trends and adapt, or better still, exploit change that really creates corporate decline and failure. As an antidote, every CEO perhaps needs to adopt a day-to-day corporate turnaround specialist approach.

7 Ideas to Rejuvenate your Business

Does your small business need a little something extra? If you have been turning over the same stable profits year after year, but aren't growing as a business then something is wrong. Success is not about having a stable, solid company. Success is about always striving to improve and grow your company whenever you can do so. If you feel as though your company has hit a wall and that it is no longer improving then, you need to take action. There are plenty of ways that you can move your business in a new direction and find new ways of expanding.

Many business owners settle for below par standards. They get all too comfortable in the day to day running of their business that they forget why they started the company in the first place. One thing all entrepreneurs have in common is a lust for money and success. Don't let these two vital things slip away from you just because you have become lazy. Instead, work hard to improve your business wherever possible.

Here are seven small business ideas for to take your business to a new direction:

1. CONSIDER A RE-BRAND

It is never too early to re-brand your business. Many business owners shy away from changing and developing their business once they have set it up. A lot of people are under the impression that re-branding alienates your current client base. In fact, a re-brand can be quite thrilling but how do you really know when should you rebrand your company? People thrive on change, and your current customers will love that you are making positive steps. Take some time to work with your staff of the re-brand. You need to capture the current zeitgeist so that you can appeal to a new-found audience. It is not about just changing the way your logo looks. It is about changing your company ideals and expanding the way you view your business. A re-brand is a dynamic way to push your company forward and expand into new areas of your market. Ensure that you do your research before making any decisions.

2. CONQUER THE INTERNET

The internet can be your best tool or your worst enemy depending on how you use it. If you don't already, you need to invest money in getting a website that promotes your company. It is vital that you get an expert to design and develop a website for you so that you know you are getting a quality product. Once you have a website, you need to find a way to drive traffic to the site. Use social media platforms to promote your website online. You should make sure that your brand has continuity on all its online accounts. Choose a tone that suits your company style and use this tone whenever communicating with customers online. An active presence on the internet will do wonders for your company's awareness. You can reach a whole new client base online at just the click of a button.

3. ADD EXTRA SERVICES TO YOUR BUSINESS

The more services you can offer your clients, the more money your company will make. Offering your customers just one product is never going to make you a large profit. Instead, look into new services or products that you can offer your existing clients. As your customers already trust you with one service, they are likely to trust you in giving them extra services. Doing so might mean that you can make more money from your existing customers straight away. For example, if your company already offers print design services, why not branch out into web design? By offering an extra service to your clients, you can make more money.

4. OPEN A SECOND PREMISES

Moving into a new area of business can also mean a literal move. Opening a second premises means that you can target a whole new group of people with your product or services. Don't hesitate in making a move to a new area, as doing so is easier than you think. Often people associate moving with stress, but opening a second premises doesn't mean that you have to worry. You only have to move some of your things, rather than the entire office. That means that you can take a gradual approach to moving. When you have a second office, you can offer much more diverse services to your customers.

5. MAKE YOUR BRAND 'TRENDY'

Making your brand trendy will make it more popular with people. Think about all the brands that people believe to be trendy. You have Apple, of course, which is a cool and young brand. Other trendy brands include Facebook, Spotify and Beats headphones. These brands are popular less for the products that they supply and more for the fact that people think they are cool. Making your brand appear young and fresh is a surefire way to expand your business. Look into what is currently popular and work from there. You might need to do some market research with young consumers to find out what makes them tick. If you can make your brand appear to be young and trendy, you can win over a whole new audience.

6. KEEP AN EYE ON YOUR COMPETITORS

Who are your direct competitors? Write a list of similar companies within your market. You need to know what these companies are doing at all times if you are going to win over their clients to switch to you. Set up Google Alerts for the opposing companies, so that whenever someone publishes a story about them you are the first to know. By finding out what your competitors are doing you can decide how best to combat them. If they offer a new service for 2021, you need to aim to offer three new services for the same year.

7. EXPORT YOUR PRODUCTS TO NEW MARKETS

If you currently only supply people in one country, it is time to expand your market. Link up with a great courier service and make your business global in an instant. The service will allow you to deliver products to people in different countries. If you have a good online presence people from new places will start to order your products. Few companies offer global delivery. If you offer that unique service, you will dominate the market.

FOUR STRATEGIES TO REJUVENATE YOUR BRAND

Spring is a great time of year to de-clutter and simplify. It's when we open the windows, clean out the closets, and rid our homes of unwanted clutter. Likewise, it's also a great time to refresh your business. Just as spring cleaning brings fresh air into a stuffy house, it can also breathe life into a company, resulting in an improved state of success.

1. DUST OFF THE COBWEBS

When your marketing goes stale, so does your business. The purpose of spring cleaning your online business is to clear away the cobwebs and stay relevant to consumers. So, what does it take to be relevant?

Stay up with the times: Take time every few months to read about new marketing tactics that can apply to your business.

Be better!: Look at what your competitors are doing online, and see if you can do it better.

Be social: Don't leave your Facebook, Twitter, or Pinterest accounts unattended for long periods of time or consumers will view you as stale, resulting in a loss of fans, followers and connections.

Appeal to the masses: Make sure the content you are posting appeals to the appropriate audience and remains cognizant of what's trending in your industry.

Strategize and Organize: Have you embraced the social media realm yet? Let's face it: Social media engagement is important for business success. However, you must be mindful of what you are posting and engaging in on social media. Social activity for the sake of activity is a waste of time. Part of spring cleaning is eliminating excess that doesn't benefit you.

If it's not relevant, appealing, or creating revenue for your company, it's not working for you. At the end of the day, your social interactions should bring a return on investment. There should always be a payoff, so there must be a sound strategy behind any social initiative. Here is one strategy you can follow:

a) Pinpoint the ultimate goal:
- What do we want from our visitors?
- What is our call to action?

Once you have a goal in mind, you can commit and act to follow through and succeed.

b) Look at your site's analytics:
- What are you doing that's working?
- What is not working?
- What could work better?

There is always room for improvement — find out what can and should be improved.

c) Look at the social analytics:
- What do Facebook or Twitter have to offer your business that you may not be taking advantage of?

Social media continues to grow, so keeping up to stay relevant is critical.

2. REFINE A FAMILIAR FOCUS: YOUR AUDIENCE

Whether you're sweeping up dust bunnies or brainstorming new business strategies, you can ask yourself these questions when reviewing your online marketing:

- What will people think about these efforts?
- How will they make people feel?
- What will people do with this information?

Your content should give your audience something to think about, something to feel good about, and something productive to do. It can appeal to urgency with a limited-time offer or appeal to kindness with a charitable campaign.

No matter what you choose to do, you must focus on how the campaign and efforts will affect your audience. Rethinking or refining your marketing plans will give your business a renewed edge.

3. REFRESH YOUR BRAND

If you are an extreme spring cleaner, you won't stop at just the kitchen or attic. You're going to fix up the entire house, top to bottom. Consider adopting this mentality for refreshing your brand as a whole. Remember these tips for improving your online business brand:

- Define what your brand currently represents: Apple, Pepsi, and McDonald's have used a variety of different slogans over the years to tailor their brand messages and stay relevant to consumers. It's part of what makes them so successful. You can do this, too.
- Be consistent in your presentation: Don't forget what you've defined from the beginning. Although your look or slogan may change, the heart of your business should remain the same.

Be willing to grow and evolve based on your vision, your audience, and your image (keeping consistency in mind).

7

REBRANDING

REBRANDING

What is Rebranding

Rebranding happens when a company changes its logo, slogan, vision, mission, values, name, target audience, or market to build a new brand identity in the minds of leads, customers, competitors, and partners. It helps brands attract new audiences, stay relevant, stand out among competitors, and improve brand awareness.

Why is rebranding important?

Your business has seven seconds to make a first impression. Sometimes brands fail to draw the attention of customers because of using the wrong logo, having a difficult or uncatchy name, or working with an unclear vision and mission.

We live in a world where trends are constantly evolving, so companies also require changes to attract new customers. This is possible with rebranding. You might just need to refresh your business, design a new logo or name after a merger with another company, or define new business objectives, mission, or vision.

So, let's consider several advantages of this process.

Benefits of Rebranding

- New Audience
- Higher Relevancy
- Improved Brand Recognition
- Improved Google Ranking
- Streamlined Teamwork

Let's review the benefits you can reap with a successful rebranding strategy.

1. NEW AUDIENCE

The main advantage of rebranding is the chance to reach a new target audience. If you focus on your company's mission, vision, values, and communicate them correctly, people will notice it.

Let's look at Old Spice. They implemented this strategy after discovering that 60% of men's body washes were purchased by women. The famous brand decided to reach female audiences with their new commercial. Their new campaign received 105 million views on YouTube, drove traffic to the brand's site, and earned 1.2 billion impressions.

2. HIGHER RELEVANCY

Rebranding allows you to keep your company up-to-date. Regardless of the age of your brand, it should always remain relevant. Companies need to move fast and follow the new trends in marketing to keep pace. As you know, design trends play an important role in how clients perceive your brand and the products you offer. Ensuring that you always stay up-to-date will help you gain customers' trust and confidence that your brand is the best.

Let's consider a successful rebranding campaign from Adidas. The company was established in 1949 and used rebranding several times to stay relevant for their customers. To connect with the millennial market, the brand stopped production of the well-known Stan Smith sneakers in 2011 and presented a refreshed version in 2014. By promoting a launch on social media and partnering with retailers and influencers, Adidas managed to capture the hearts of their new audience and boost sales.

3. IMPROVED BRAND RECOGNITION

Humanizing your brand through a genuine story or video during rebranding can make your company stay in the minds of your clients. Research shows that customers are more likely to engage with a company that delivers an experience, matches their views, or evokes specific emotions.

For example, Dos Equis, a Mexican beer manufacturer decided to change its branding story. This company created "The Most Interesting Man in the World" campaign with a clever and powerful story. The commercial was catchy, well thought out, and humorous. As a result, beer sales increased by 22%.

4. IMPROVED GOOGLE RANKING

Considering the fact that SEO ranks second in the highest ROI list after email marketing, investing in your company to build a strong brand is the right decision. If customers engage with your new brand and recognize it, you can be sure that Google will evaluate your efforts. For example, after serious brand building, Neil Patel's website traffic went from 240,839 to 454,382 users in several months.

5. STREAMLINED TEAMWORK

If your company doesn't have a clearly defined mission, vision, and strategies, you have a chance to restructure them according to your needs. This structural clarity is critical to improving the efficiency of your business: hire the right employees and make them work accurately, manage company operations, and make the right business decisions.

It is essential to be aware of the pros of a rebranding campaign. Additionally, it is important to know in which situations you should consider this risky move.

When do you need rebranding?

Rebranding is a complicated and costly process that carries big risks for big and small companies alike. Therefore, you should have serious reasons to implement this method in your business. Here are the main reasons to consider rebranding:

- **IF THERE IS A MARKET REPOSITIONING:**

Repositioning involves changing a company's existing brand or product status in the marketplace. This process is critical when a company has a weak or outdated image, requires global strategic changes, or needs a new target audience. If you decide to reposition your product to target a completely new market segment through new packaging, size, taste, promotional channels, price, or place, it is advisable to think about rebranding.

- **WHEN YOU WANT TO IMPROVE YOUR COMPANY'S REPUTATION:**

A scandal on social media, low quality of products, or data leaks can result in a tarnished reputation. Of course, it has a negative impact on your company and its customers. Real changes within the company can help eliminate negative associations that arise in the minds of people and win customers' trust again.

- **IF A COMPANY MERGER TAKES PLACE:**

If two companies link forces and become one, you have a merger. To showcase the best qualities of each business, gain customers' trust, develop brand awareness, and avoid confusion, a refresh is necessary.

A merger allows your company to enter new markets, use financial resources efficiently, obtain more profit, new management, and more. This process also influences consumers as it results in better customer service, higher quality products, and lower prices.

- **WHEN YOU WANT TO GO INTERNATIONAL:**

When a business enters international markets, it often resorts to rebranding to achieve distinctive growth and financial gains. To connect with new locations, companies come up with a new company name and a logo that identifies your brand is unique, easy to remember, and can be understood in other countries.

- **IF THERE IS A CHANGE IN LEADERSHIP:**

Companies are linked to their leaders. If a brand changes hands to an outside owner, a new identity is a way to emphasize the transition.

Remember not to make changes just because you're bored with your logo or slogan, or you're looking for attention because your brand awareness efforts didn't meet all your expectations. You are misleading yourself if you think that a branding change is the fastest and easiest way to improve your business.

To successfully implement this strategy, you need to study the types of rebranding strategies that are available and choose the one that suits you the most.

Types of Rebranding

1. Partial Rebranding
2. Total Rebrand

Before getting started, you need to determine which type of rebranding strategy you need.

1. PARTIAL REBRANDING

This strategy is used when you decide to add something new to your current brand without totally changing it. A refresh is necessary when your company's logo and image have become outdated or there has been a slight shift in your business objectives.

2. TOTAL REBRAND

This option is used when your company has had a foundational shift like mergers, a change in leadership, product overhauls, etc. As a result, your brand needs to undergo a change in brand identity along with your brand mission, vision, and values. Here comes a complete makeover.

The gaming hardware manufacturer, Oculus, was acquired by Facebook in 2017. Shortly after the acquisition, Facebook did some rebranding, and critics of the merger feel that the changes to the logo were just the beginning for Facebook's total rebranding of Oculus.

Now that you know the main types of rebranding, let's consider the steps to get started.

How to rebrand a company

- Redefine your target audience and market
- Rethink your vision, mission, and values
- Reconsider your company name
- Revise your brand slogan
- Re-establish your brand identity

Once you've decided whether you need a partial or a total rebranding strategy, take a closer look at the following steps to implement this strategy in your business.

1. Redefine your target audience and market

Conduct research to understand your target audience, what your competitors are doing, what is unique about your brand, and how it differs from other companies in the same industry.

In-depth research that involves focus groups and data analysis, allows you to notice if your customers and competitors don't match your idea. Identify your actual buyers and their preferences. Compare this data with your initial target market and audience to find out some differences. As soon as you manage to define your actual market and audience, you can go forward in implementing your strategy.

2. RETHINK YOUR VISION, MISSION, AND VALUES

Every company has three main elements that you need to evaluate: mission, vision, and values. Analyze each of them to understand what is going wrong.

Vision: Vision gives your brand direction and defines the actions your company needs to take. Over time, the vision of your business might change, and that is totally normal. However, it is essential to redefine your vision as soon as this happens to ensure that your employees are moving in the right direction and make decisions accordingly.

Mission: This defines the purpose of your company. Your mission describes your primary consumers, the products you produce, and your location. It is your business' roadmap. As your mission changes, your messaging requires change,too.

Values: Your company's values explain why you're working towards your vision, and why you're committed to your mission. As brands evolve, they might change their old values. So you need to reflect your new values to show your main focus.

Remember, if the components mentioned above change, the way you communicate them to your audience will also requires some change. The language choice, the tone, and voice have to match the message you want to convey.

3. RECONSIDER YOUR COMPANY NAME

Of course, changing a company's name is a serious step as it can cost you brand recognition and organic traffic. However, if you are seriously thinking about changing your brand's name, make sure that you have a plan of recovery after you rebrand.

In general, if your company name still aligns with your mission, vision, and values, it is better to keep it. Yet if it mismatches your identity, it is advisable to modify it. Make sure that your new brand name conveys your message, is easy-to-spell and catchy. The right name also supports your goals and business growth.

4. REVISE YOUR BRAND SLOGAN

Your aim here is to create a slogan that communicates your company mission, vision, and is also memorable. Consider changing it carefully as it highlights the purpose of your brand.

For sure, customers remember catchy slogans from famous brands like "Just do it" from Nike, "I'm Lovin' It" from McDonald's, or "Because You're Worth It" from L'Oreal. To create a great slogan, consider providing instructions, making a claim, getting metaphorical, or using poetic language.

To help you create a great slogan for your brand, here are several simple tips:

- keep it short, simple, and clear;
- use your unique value proposition;
- be consistent;
- ensure that it can stand the test of time;
- consider your target audience and market.

5. RE-ESTABLISH YOUR BRAND IDENTITY

There are several things you might consider changing about your company's brand identity like your logo, shapes, imagery, colors, or guidelines. Here are several changes you need.

1. Change your logo:

If you have had some internal changes in your company and you want to demonstrate them, consider developing a new logo. To refresh your old logo, use these basics to do it correctly:

- demonstrate your confidence by creating a simple logo;
- create a logo that will stand out;
- use universal shapes and styles that fit your communication channels;

- ensure that your new logo supports your mission, vision, and values in the long run;
- try to use parts of your old logo to help customers recognize your brand.
- Use different colors

According to a study, color raises brand recognition by 80%. So, color influences your customers and your brand.

Look at your company colors with fresh eyes to decide whether it matches your brand image. Besides, nowadays it is essential to check how your color palette looks on-screen and in-print. Make sure it looks the same on different brand materials.

2. Reconsider your Shapes and imagery:

Once you decide to change any visual elements of your branding, give a thought to modifying shapes and imagery to keep everything cohesive. Also, make sure that your imagery and shapes support your brand's message.

5 Reasons Why Branding Success Is Important For Small Business

STRONG RE-BRANDING HELPS YOUR MARKETING

Small businesses make the mistake of thinking branding success is only achievable by big businesses. While big businesses have more money to spend on things like logos and website design, all businesses need to dedicate time to building their own brand. Your business is a brand whether you think so or not, and branding can make or break a business today.

Think of brands from your childhood. You likely remember brands like Disney or Coca-Cola clearly, and they bring along strong associations. This is good branding, and you can do the same thing with your own business! No matter how big or small your business is, you should have a brand strategy! Let's talk about the 5 reasons why branding success is important for small business!

1. STORYTELLING:

Stories are what connect you with your customers. Sure, your logo and color selection matters, but not nearly as much as the story you share. Psychology today points out the ways consumers are influenced by emotions. While we'd all like to think we're rational, logical purchasers, we probably base most of our emotions on how we feel. Emotions lead to preferences and this is how we make our decisions. Branding that uses emotion to tell a story connects with audiences on a new level!

2. RECOGNITION:

Consumers are bombarded with different brands every day. Most of these brands come and go quickly in our lives, and we don't even take the time to notice them. With so many different brands to choose from today, how do you stand out? Strong branding is easy to recognize!

Have you ever gone shopping and had to choose between two different brands? You probably chose the brand you recognize whether you realized it or not. Brand recognition is a powerful tool! By building a brand consumers can easily and quickly recognize, you're likely to land more sales!

3. TRUST:

Consumers use brands they trust. Having a strong brand is like making a promise to consumers. You're setting a level of quality with your brand, and consumers know if they engage with your brand, they can expect that same level of quality. Social proof, customer service, and strong messaging all lead to building trust! Trust in your brand is step one for brand success!

4. MOTIVATE EMPLOYEES:

Hiring employees is one thing but motivating them is another. When employees can recognize your brand, your mission, and your message, it's easier for them to support your cause! Employees like to feel they're a part of something exciting. A strong brand gives them something to feel pride in which ultimately leads to greater motivation! There's a clear link between branding success and employee engagement!

5. PROGRESS:

You might know where your business is now, but do you know where you'll take it in the future? Branding creates a roadmap for your business that propels it into tomorrow. You'll know how to create products for your business whether you're trying to launch a new product or print custom t-shirts. You'll know how to communicate with your customers and employees. Most importantly, you'll achieve branding success by knowing your own story as a business!

8

SUCCESS

SUCCESS

Congratulations!!!!

If you are reading this chapter,

That's evidence that you are truly serious about this thing of ours and you are well on your way to……. Success ({laughs} which is the chapter we are in right now)

This book is as previously mentioned is dedicated to my late cousin Don Tuzo. I remember being in his living room in Las Vegas, trying to think of a tagline for a company I was preparing to start. I began to envision the future and what I wanted it to look like. I have always been one to operate on my terms, I don't wish for things, I will things into existence. I do not make resolutions at the beginning of the year, I mind map a strategic plan to accomplish what I want. I believe sincerely on the power of words. So then it hit me, Precise Business Group, Inc., "Redefining Success"

What Defines a Successful Business?

Every entrepreneur wants to run a successful business, but it can be hard to define what that means. Just keeping your doors open? Inventing the product that beats global warming? Becoming a millionaire? A billionaire? Some business owners jump in with no clear idea of what they'd consider a successful business, but achieving your dreams will be easier if you nail down exactly what they are.

Tip

Typical measures of business success include the growth of your company, the money it provides you, or your ability to keep control of the business for yourself or your children. There's no one standard because entrepreneurs don't all enter business for the same reason. Choosing your own definition of a successful business is the best path to satisfaction.

Defining Success

One of the first things to get clear in your mind is whether your most important value is liquidity, growth or control. Prioritizing the growth of your business could be a matter of ambition, or that it increases the benefits you think you can bring to society. Liquidity allows you take money out of the company to finance your lifestyle, or to donate to charity. If control is your top priority, you should avoid steps that benefit the company at the cost of your control of the business.

Once you know what you want, think about the metrics you'll use to measure it. There are lots of financial standards you can use to measure whether you're a successful business, so narrow it down to a few relevant benchmarks. For instance, you can measure successful liquidity by how much cash you want from the company to finance the other parts of your life. If control is your priority, comparing debt to earnings can show if you risk losing control to your creditors.

There are other, personal aspects of entrepreneurship you should think about. Does success include passing your business on to your kids? How much do you want company operations to align with your personal values? Are there lines of business you'd have moral objections to entering, even if they were profitable? The better you understand your definition of a successful business, the better you can shape your policy to fit.

Think about what kind of successful work life would make you happy. One of the definitions for a winner in business is that they wake up excited that they're doing a job they love. Even if the tasks for the day are challenging, the thought of tackling them should be energizing, not intimidating.

Making a Plan

Success takes hard work, persistence and planning. Once you've figured out what's important to you, start drawing up a plan.

Set one-, five- and 10-year goals. Based on your definition of success, where do you want your business to be? How close will you be to achieving your vision?

Research your industry. How realistic are your goals in the context of your competitive environment? If you're a small-town baker, becoming the tops in your local industry might be realistic. Knocking Disney or Microsoft off their perch is much less so.

Are your goals SMART — that is, Specific, Measurable, Attainable, Relevant and Timed? If not, work to make them so. If your goals aren't specific and measurable, for instance, it'll be hard to tell if you're achieving them or not.

Once you have a definition of success and a list of goals tied to them, think about the steps to achieve them (we have discussed step by step building blocks to achieve these in previous chapters). Delegate some of that work to your team. It's quite possible there are parts of your plan that you can't do yourself — tech work, say, or marketing — so share your vision with the people who have the skills. Divide up and assign the goals in whatever way makes the most sense for you and your company. Everyone at your business should be on board with your vision.

Movement and Measurement

Setting goals and determining your direction aren't enough. To become a successful business owner, you have to check back regularly and see how you're meeting whatever metrics you've set for your company. Any review process that works is good, so long as you apply it regularly. Look at whether you've met your goals, and whether you've met them on time. If you've fallen short, you need to know how far short, and where you went wrong. Once you know, course-correct.

One of the standard business tips is that you should review your long-range plans every year. Don't just look at how well you're doing on your goals, ask yourself if you still believe in them. Perhaps when you started your company, growth was your top priority, but now you'd like more liquidity so that you can enjoy your leisure time more. Perhaps greater experience shows you some of your ambitions simply aren't attainable.

There's nothing wrong with changing your goals if they no longer work for you. Sit down, repeat the goal planning progress and come up with a new agenda full of SMART goals that work for where you are now. Nobody but you gets to define your success, and you can change the definition if you choose.

If you're still committed to your goals and your review shows you're achieving them, take time for a celebration like we discussed in chapter 1. Compliment and reward yourself, and do the same for your staff. Winning is something to take pride in, and acknowledging success helps give everyone energy as you head off for the next benchmark.

5 Secrets to Success in Business

Business is hard, but if you put in the work and keep a positive mindset you will succeed.

I often wonder what the secret to success is, especially as it relates to business. At the end of the day, it all stands to reason, we're all in this struggle. A rat race, if you will. Constantly fighting an uphill battle. Often, we feel frustrated. Sometimes, defeated. But, what if I told you that the secrets to success in business aren't as complicated as many make them out to be?

Okay, coming from me, those words might not have the same impact. But, what if I told you that this information comes directly from two of the best salespeople on the planet? As a student of self-improvement, I've followed many of the world's most sought-after purveyors of success. Anthony Robbins, for one. He's definitely my hero. But, so is Zig Ziglar.

If the name Zig Ziglar doesn't ring a bell, then you might have been hiding under a rock for the past few decades. He's touched the lives of over 250 million people around the planet. Sold millions of books. And most certainly created thousands of millionaires. Now, while Ziglar might no longer be among the living, his words most certainly live on.

Ziglar coined iconic quotes that are often referenced today in business. Things like, "Your attitude, not your aptitude, will determine your altitude." Along with, "What you get by achieving your goals is not as important as what you become by achieving your goals." And, "You were born to win, but to be a winner, you must plan to win, prepare to win, and expect to win." Plus so much more.

These are age-old adages. Sure to last generations upon generations to come. So if there was one person in particular to ask about the secrets to success in business, a person who I could speak to today, it was Harrington. Over the past 30 years, he's helped launch over 500 products. Those products have generated well north of $5 billion in sales. As one of the original sharks on the Shark Tank, he's also the father of the infomercial.

How to Sell Anything to Anyone

There are so many facets to sales. I talk about sales because it's the foundation for success. To succeed, you have to know how to sell. Hands down, it's the most important skill you can have. Everything revolves around sales. If you're no good at sales, you'll have a hard time succeeding in business.

Sales is about influence. There are methods of persuasion that work very well in business. But, there are also several fundamentals that need to be in place if you want to succeed. If those fundamentals aren't in place, you can pretty much kiss your chances for success goodbye.

So let's just call them secrets. Sure, they're fundamental. But, they're also categorically secret. Not in the terms of nobody knowing or understanding them. More so, people simply overlook them.

Not convinced that sales is the basis for success? Just imagine for a moment what you're selling at any given moment. No, I'm not talking about products or services or information. I'm talking about selling yourself. You need to sell yourself at just about any point if you want to succeed:

- You need to sell a good college on why you would be a great fit
- You need to sell your skills to a potential employer to get a good job
- You need to sell a potential spouse or date on why they should be with you
- You need to sell your parents on why they should give you an allowance
- You need to sell your bank on why they should give you a mortgage
- You need to sell a landlord on why you would be a good tenant

Selling is everything. Everything! Hands down. Now, selling without holding steadfast to a variety of so-called secrets doesn't guarantee your long-term success. Sure, you'll make some short-term progress, but not strides. There won't be exponential growth.

5 Secrets to Success in Business

If sales are the basis to success in business, what are the secrets to succeeding at sales? At the foundation of any business, there are quite literally five fundamental keys that you need to have in place. This is not just about building an irresistible offer. Yes, you need that. But, you need so much more in place before that's even concocted or created.

While there are likely dozens, if not hundreds, of secrets to success, these five are crucial. If you follow these, you can navigate your way to success in the long term. Not in the short term. Remember, this is about consistency in your approach. It's not about faltering or giving up or making excuses. It's about staying on the straight and narrow.

1. CREATE SOMETHING OF REAL VALUE:

Value is the cornerstone to success. If you stopped to think about it right now, the richest people in the world have created the most value. Hands down, it's crucial if you're looking to win. So why is value so important you ask?

While some people might be able to sell anything, that doesn't guarantee long-term success. If you put your own needs first before the consumer's, you'll lose. Whatever you sell, manufacture, create or dream up, do it with the consumer's best interests at heart. In other words, add insane amounts of value.

Think about this for a moment. Before most of the world's most successful companies ever made a dime, they added value first. Facebook connected the world through a massive social network. Google provided the most uncannily accurate search results before it ever enabled you to run an ad, and so on.

2. IMPROVE THE LIVES OF OTHERS:

Not only should you deliver real value, but you should look for ways that you can improve the lives of others with whatever it is that you're peddling. Sure, you could sell anything to anyone for a brief period. But, if you're not improving the lives of consumers, you're really wasting your time.

By building products, services or providing information that improves the lives of others, you can quite literally transform your business and catapult it into the stratosphere. We're talking long-term exponential growth. Beyond anything that you could quite possibly dream of.

That doesn't mean you can't profit from your efforts. It simply means that you have to focus on improving the consumer's life first and foremost. That's the key or the secret to success here. Focus on that and watch as your business takes shape and reaches new heights. Ignore it, and watch it crash and burn.

3. BE AUTHENTIC AND TRANSPARENT

No one likes a sleazeball. You can't sell anything. Don't be that guy (or girl) that people dread speaking to. The used car salesman. The underhanded low-balling greedy saleswoman. Don't be that person. Just don't. Instead, if you really want to succeed, you should be authentic and transparent.

Don't make unrealistic claims. People can see right through it. Instead, be honest about what your product or service or information will do. Use real-world reviews from people who've tested whatever it is that you're offering. Those testimonials go a long way.

Whether you're audience is millennial or baby-boomers, everyone can tell when you're being inauthentic. People aren't stupid. So don't take advantage of them by trying to be or say something that's not true. It's just a waste of time.

4. FOCUS ON POSITIVITY

While you shouldn't look to please everyone all the time, you should focus your thoughts on positivity. In other words, don't think negative thoughts. Yes, it's hard. But, it's necessary. If you begin to veer off to the realm of negativity, your entire life follows.

Considering that we have upwards of 60,000 thoughts per day and a large degree of those happen in the subconscious mind, if you don't focus your thoughts on positivity, you'll feel like you aren't in control.

You won't be in control of your destiny. And you certainly won't be able to make sales when you're in that headspace.

This is one of the important pieces of advice for entrepreneur. You simply can't make progress if you're always focusing on pain rather than the pleasure of a positive outcome. Sure, business is hard. We all know that. But, it gets easier with time as long as you put in the work and keep a positive mindset.

5. FOLLOW THE 80-20 RULE

The 80-20 Rule states that 80 percent of the results come from 20 percent of the efforts. In sales, this means that 80 percent of the sales come from 20 percent of the customers. It also means that, within the 20 percent of efforts, another 80-20 Rule applies. That translates to a very small amount of efforts leading to a very large amount of results.

Focus on that. Find the efforts that are producing the biggest results. This isn't about working long and unending days, toiling away or being the last one to always leave the office. This is about productivity. If you can find what works, you can scale it out. Think 4 Hour Work Week rather than 18-hour day.

Too many people think that the secret to success lies in working yourself to the bone. It doesn't. Just identify what efforts are producing the biggest results and scale. That's how you seriously scale out and grow any business.

Citations

1. Forbes. "The 7 Success Principles of Steve Jobs." Accessed June 1, 2021.
2. Forbes. "Steve Jobs: 'People With Passion Can Change The World'." Accessed June 1, 2021.
3. Carmine Gallo. "The Storyteller's Secret: From TED Speakers to Business Page 15. Macmillan, 2016.
4. David Kirkpatrick. "The Facebook Effect: The Inside Story of the Company That Is Connecting the World." Simon and Schuster, 2011.
5. CNBC. "Warren Buffet's Secret "10 Ways to Get Rich" Hits Hundreds of Sunday Newspapers." Accessed June 1, 2021.

Shawn M. Nicholson, Entrpreneur
L3 Publishing House

Shawn M. Nicholson is a Pastor, serial entrepreneur, community advocate, and servant leader. As an executive with over 25- years of proven leadership, management, organizational and problem-solving skills, he is a recognized and sought-after thought leader on faith-based business development, and workforce development for youth and young adults. Mr. Nicholson is a community connector and an innovative and strategic leader with a passion for working in partnership with Black and Brown communities to eradicate generational poverty and stimulate economic prosperity for those who have been most excluded from it.

During the past 25 years, he has developed and maintained several thriving businesses including Beautiful Temple Ministries, a community-rooted church ministry that was centered on loving people to life, Precise Business Group, Inc, a company that provides vocational training, workforce development and staffing. Additionally, there is a license training arm for the American Red Cross, the (NAT) Nurses Assistant Training Program, which is the flagship program. This program prepares individuals that desire to enter into the healthcare field by preparing them to sit for the state board exam. PBG has helped mentor and mold over 125 participants since September 2020. New Ventures New Visions, objective is to assist women in starting businesses that create sustainable employment. BTM Properties and Development, LLC, and a host of others. He currently serves as the Principal & Founder of SMN Square Inc., a company that provides the building blocks for sustainability and success through executive coaching and leadership development. SMN Square, Inc., has developed an (AED) method and is very passionate and dedicated in helping individuals attain economic independence by **Assisting** businesses, **encouraging** entrepreneurship and **Developing** ecosystem builders.

Additionally, recently Shawn M. Nicholson was contracted to spearhead and lead workforce development in the Crater Region, which consists of five cities and four counties that covers the most economically disenfranchised communities in the Commonwealth of Virginia. He most recently applied his passion for workforce development and community development towards emergency hiring over 200 community members from across Virginia's hardest hit communities by the pandemic, to educate and vaccinate their neighbors in Black and Brown communities, against the destructive Covid-19 disease.

In 2007, Nicholson was led to start an outreach ministry in his hometown of Richmond, VA and that evolved to planting a church. Some of the highlights include a weekly partnership with Richmond Friends of the Homeless. They would provide hot meals once a week and various wrap around services for the homeless and working poor. A few of the program's successes were feeding between 400-600 individuals a month. Helping the children with school supplies and free haircuts.

Shawn M. Nicholson's passion and desire to help support the community was shown through the adoption of an area apartment community after a homicide had occurred and the body was found in the parking lot of the church. Nicholson assisted in coordinating the police, businesses, other churches and individuals and formed a neighborhood coalition. A few successes from this effort were, tutoring programs, training, they were able to bring the local banks in and set up bank accounts for the Hispanic community due to a series of robberies.

More community efforts continued with the starting of a chapter for the Girls Scouts of America. The first meeting enrolled 65 young ladies. Starting a flag football team with the neighborhood young men that participated in competitive play with other churches throughout the city. A summer feeding program that fed hot meals to over 200 children a day and over 75 returning citizens in the afternoons. This program also employed over 25 individuals with part time work for the summer.

Shawn Nicholson also held the position of 1st Vice President for the Newport News Chapter of (NAN), National Action Network. One of the highlights of this position was an education rally and partnership with the University of Phoenix and Rev. Al Sharpton.

Shawn M. Nicholson also owns the trade for L3 Life, Legend, Legacy and PASS-I-ON. He has taken the word "passion" and broken it up into three words: Pass, I, On. His desire is to pass on what he has learned and experienced onto as many individuals as possible. He believes that God is the source of all of his accomplishments and his desire is to build a legacy that will last for generations to come. He believes that passion is simply the ability to PASS-I-ON.

www.ingramcontent.com/pod-product-compliance
Ingram Content Group UK Ltd.
Pitfield, Milton Keynes, MK11 3LW, UK
UKHW021307180426
11947UKWH00015B/1074